This is a fictionalised biography describing some of the key moments (so far!) in the career of Virgil van Dijk.

Some of the events described in this book are based upon the author's imagination and are probably not entirely accurate representations of what actually happened.

Tales from the Pitch
Van Dijk
by Harry Coninx

Published in the United State of America and Canada
by Leapfrog Press
www.leapfrogpress.com

Distributed in the United States by
Consortium Book Sales and Distribution
St Paul, Minnesota 55114
www.cbsd.com

First Published in the United Kingdom by Raven Books
An imprint of Ransom Publishing Ltd.
Unit 7, Brocklands Farm, West Meon, Hampshire GU32 1JN, UK
www.ransom.co.uk

ISBN 978-1-948585-80-4
Also available as an eBook
First published in the United States 2025

Copyright © 2023 Ransom Publishing Ltd.
Text copyright © 2023 Ransom Publishing Ltd.
Cover illustration by Ben Farr © 2023 Ben Farr

All rights reserved under International and Pan-American Copyright Conventions

All rights reserved. No part of this publication may be reproduced, stored in a retrieval system, or transmitted, in any form or by any means, electronic, mechanical, photocopying, recording or otherwise, without the prior permission of the publishers.

The rights of Harry Coninx to be identified as the author and of Ben Farr to be identified as the illustrator of this Work have been asserted by them in accordance with sections 77 and 78 of the Copyright, Design and Patents Act 1988.

TALES FROM THE PITCH

VIRGIL VAN DIJK

HARRY CONINX

Leapfrog Press
New York and London

*For my dog, Chester, who is as big as Virgil
and is just as good a defender*

CONTENTS

		Page
1	Kings of Europe	7
2	Growing Up Fast	13
3	Willem II	17
4	Dreams and Dishes	21
5	Groningen	26
6	The Attacking Defender	32
7	Heroes	38
8	Not Here	41
9	Recovery	47
10	Old Friends, New Plans	50
11	Decisions	54
12	Celtic	58
13	Reality Check	63
14	The Booking	67
15	A Great Result	72
16	Word from Southampton	75
17	The Call-Up	78
18	Saint Virgil	82
19	Virgil's Revenge	86
20	The Record-Breaking Reds	90
21	A Dream Debut	94
22	Championship Chances	98
23	Right Behind You	103
24	The Impossible	107
25	The Best Player in Europe	113

1
KINGS OF EUROPE

June 2019, Wanda Metropolitano Stadium, Madrid, Spain
Champions League Final, Tottenham v Liverpool

The brilliant white of Tottenham's shirts seared the corner of Virgil's eye as he forced himself to look ahead.

Lined up just next to him in the tunnel of Atlético Madrid's Wanda Metropolitano stadium he could see Kane, Eriksen, Lloris ... the list went on. These were the kinds of players he'd only dreamt of going up against all those years ago at Willem II.

His head spun at the thought, so he tried to focus on what his captain was saying.

"Come on, lads! Let's do it this year!" Jordan Henderson roared.

To anyone else in the tunnel, Virgil looked his normal, relaxed self, but in reality his stomach was tightening into knots. He fiercely wanted this for himself, for his team, and for the tens of thousands of Liverpool fans waiting just outside.

Joël Matip, Virgil's central defensive partner, glanced back over his shoulder and gave Virgil a little nod.

Virgil acknowledged him with a small smile, before determinedly putting one foot in front of the other and making his way on to the pitch.

Only 12 months ago Liverpool had been beaten 3-1 by Real Madrid. Now, back in Madrid, here they were with another chance of winning the Champions League.

In one moment the familiar anthem was booming out over the stadium, then an instant later the whistle had gone and Virgil was getting his first touch. The feel of the ball against his boot was electrifying and his nerves instantly disappeared.

It wasn't long before he spotted the ball in the air and had to run to it at full pelt. He saw a white shirt running in the same direction. The Tottenham player was quick, but Virgil was quicker. Using all the muscles in his legs to launch himself into the air, Virgil made good contact with the ball and headed it straight to his team-mate.

Safely back on the ground, he caught a glimpse of the guy he'd just beaten in the air. On the back of the shirt, Virgil made out four letters:

KANE

Turning back to the game, Virgil saw his team-mate Sadio Mané bursting into the box with the ball. Sadio cut inside and tried a cross that was blocked by Sissoko.

From where he was standing Virgil couldn't see the ball hit Sissoko, but he suddenly saw the other players appealing for handball.

Instinctively, he raised his arms as well and looked over to the referee.

PENALTY!

Virgil shouted a word of encouragement to Salah, as the Egyptian striker stepped up to take it. Together with the fans in the stadium and those watching at home, Virgil held his breath.

Salah smashed it to the right and the ball shot past Lloris and into the back of the net. The Liverpool fans sprang to their feet to celebrate their early lead.

Motivated by their fans' cheers, Liverpool pushed hard, but Tottenham were putting up a good fight. This was an ideal game for a defender like Virgil. He won every tackle, blocked every shot and beat every Tottenham player in the air.

By half-time a second goal still hadn't come. Liverpool manager Jürgen Klopp didn't say much in the dressing room. He knew the players understood the importance of the game and that, in this match, one goal just wasn't enough.

Back on the pitch, Tottenham were seeing more possession and were really testing Virgil. When Heung-Min Son started running at him, it took every ounce of his strength and pace to win the ball back.

Then, only minutes later, the ball fell to Lucas Moura in the box. Virgil could only turn and watch as the Tottenham striker fired an effort at the Liverpool goal.

Alisson threw himself at the ball and managed to scramble it to safety. Relief surged through Virgil's body and he took a deep breath. They could still do this.

With 10 minutes left to play, Liverpool won a corner. Virgil got the nod from the manager to head up with Matip.

The corner ball was headed back up into the air and Virgil saw it coming towards him. He tilted his body and tried to volley it towards the goal.

He missed the ball entirely, and for a split-second his heart sunk at his mistake.

But there was no time to dwell on it – the ball was back in the air.

Virgil flung himself towards it, desperate to knock it back into the penalty area. He felt his head get a slight connection and, as he turned, he saw the ball at the feet of the substitute, Divock Origi.

The Belgian striker swivelled and sank the ball into the bottom corner of the net.

GOAL!

Virgil threw his arms up in celebration and sprinted towards the corner flag.

The stadium had erupted with the cheers of the tens of thousands of Liverpool fans who'd made the journey.

Moments later it was confirmed: Liverpool had won 2-0.

As Virgil jogged around the pitch, embracing his team-mates and sharing the moment with the fans, all the while smiling from ear to ear, he tried to take in the atmosphere so he could remember this moment for the rest of his life.

He was at the heart of the best team in Europe. They were now Champions League winners and, as for Virgil – he was only just getting started.

2
GROWING UP FAST

June 2008
Virgil's childhood home in Breda, the Netherlands

"Mum, I seriously don't think I can go." Virgil groaned as he lay stretched out on the sofa. At six-foot-three he filled the little two-seater, even when he was curled up.

Hellen leaned around the door frame and cast a concerned look over her teenage son. Day by day, she had watched him grow at a quite alarming rate over the past few months.

When he had first complained about the throbbing pains in his legs, she'd thought he was just trying to get out of work that evening, or was trying to avoid cleaning his room.

She quickly realised this wasn't the case when the pains made him miss one of his training sessions at Willem. Playing football – and his position in the reserve team at that club – meant everything to him. If he was missing training, the pains were bad.

"I know it hurts, Virg, but growing pains always pass. They'll be over soon. Unless you're planning on just bursting through our roof one day!"

Virgil was too busy trying to adjust the way he was lying on the sofa to respond. He would do anything to find a comfortable position that stopped the dull ache in his bones.

"Maybe it *is* best you take a few days off."

He winced at the words. The longer he missed practice at Willem, the more nervous he felt.

Even before needing to take all this time off, he'd heard rumours that the manager, Edwin Hermans, wasn't convinced that he had much potential. One of the coaches had even tipped Virgil off that Edwin had been saying he had too many 'limitations'. And besides, Virgil just missed kicking a ball about. If he could, he'd be doing it every minute of every day.

His mum's voice brought him back to the present moment.

"Can you stand up for me, Virg. I might give the doctor a ring and give him an update. He said to let him know if you were still growing steadily."

Wincing, Virgil pulled himself to his feet. He towered above his mother, who picked up a tape measure from the table.

Climbing on to the sofa, she carefully held the tape measure against his long body and flattened his curls against the top of his head.

When she finally managed to take a measurement, she looked at the number and couldn't believe what she was seeing. She squinted at it, hoping that if she stared at it for long enough, the numbers might change.

They didn't.

"Well ... that means ... you've grown 16 centimetres in the last few months."

They looked at each other in disbelief.

"It'll pass, Virgil," Hellen repeated, taking her son's hand and giving it a reassuring squeeze.

3
WILLEM II

February 2010
Willem II reserve ground, Tilburg

A Willem II striker raced in on goal, accelerating away from the opposition's defenders. He faced down the goalkeeper, looking certain to score, when a long leg appeared out of nowhere. It was followed by the rest of Virgil van Dijk's body, as he slid in front of the striker and away to the left, taking the ball with him.

Back on his feet, Virgil saw the striker storming

towards him, desperate to win the ball back. With a quick shimmy, Virgil flicked the ball around the striker's wild lunge and started sprinting towards the half-way line. He heard ripples of applause from some of the thirty-odd people watching.

His growth spurt from nearly a year ago had seen him grow 18 centimeters in a short time, and everyone was impressed to see how well he'd settled into his new form.

"Virgil! Out wide!"

Virgil pinged the ball over the heads of the opposition defenders, straight to the feet of his waiting team-mate, who took on a defender, skipped past him and whipped the ball across the penalty area.

An onrushing striker met it with his head and the ball skidded off the wet grass, under the diving goalkeeper and into the net.

Virgil jogged to the corner to join his team-mates in celebration. It had been a difficult game in torrential rain, and he was glad it was done. That goal made it 2-0 and sealed the win for the Willem II Academy side.

At the end of the game the ref blew his whistle and the two teams shook hands, but even on the winning side there were few happy faces. The first team were playing the next day and every Willem II player was disappointed to have been left out.

Virgil trudged off the pitch and headed towards the dressing room.

"Hey! Virgil! Wait up!"

He turned and saw his manager, Edwin, striding towards him across the muddy pitch. He looked annoyed.

"What was that out there?" Edwin bellowed, gesturing towards the pitch.

A look of confusion spread across Virgil's face.

"You could have cost us the game back there!"

"Me? I stopped him, didn't I?"

"Yeah, but you were miles out of position. You play like that in the big league and you'll get torn apart! You can't just rely on your pace to get yourself back."

Virgil frowned and looked down at his feet. He couldn't believe it. He'd tried harder than anybody else in that game, and now he was getting shouted at.

"Look, Virgil," Edwin continued. "You want to play at the highest level, don't you? The Champions League? The World Cup?"

Virgil nodded.

"Then you need to learn these things."

4
DREAMS AND DISHES

June 2010

Local restaurant in Breda

"Watch it, kid!"

Virgil felt a strong forearm in his back and he stumbled forwards, as one of the chefs charged past him. It was a Tuesday night and he was three hours into his dishwashing shift at a restaurant in Breda.

The owner, Bram, was making his way towards him with a stack of plates in his arms.

"Incoming!" he announced cheerfully, as he dumped the dirty dishes next to the sink.

It was a depressing sight for Virgil. Willem were yet to offer him a professional contract and, with no interest from any other clubs, it was looking as though his football career was going to be over before it had even begun.

"Don't look so glum, Virgil," Bram chuckled, slapping the seventeen-year-old on the back. "You hear anything from Ajax?"

Virgil took the top plate off the pile and dropped it into the washing-up bowl, watching it sink below the bubbles.

"Not yet, boss. It's starting to look like I'll be here my whole life, washing dishes."

Bram laughed.

"Oh, chin up, son. I've seen you play and I've never seen anything like it! This kid's gonna be a superstar – aren't I right, boys?" he shouted to nobody in particular.

A couple of the boys dotted about the kitchen nodded, but most said nothing.

Bram leaned in to Virgil and spoke in a more serious tone. "Honestly kid, I really think you're going to be OK."

As Bram charged back out to clear more tables, Virgil went back to scrubbing the dishes and entertaining himself as he always did – by thinking about football.

He imagined himself on a pitch, with fans chanting his name as he stole the ball from a striker and sped away.

And then, in his imagination, he could vividly see himself holding up a major trophy. He wasn't sure whether it was the Champions League or the World Cup, but he knew it was one of those two.

The sound of his boss's voice yanked him out of his daydreams and back to the sink in front of him.

"Virgil's just back here, Martin. Trust me, he's a superstar ... Yeah, as good as Terry, probably better!"

Bram was back in the kitchen now, struggling to get past everyone and dragging with him a man who looked completely baffled.

"Virgil, this is Martin Koeman. He's a scout at

Groningen. You might know him – his sons are quite famous!"

Virgil couldn't believe it. Ronald Koeman had been one of his heroes growing up – and here he was shaking hands with Ronald's dad.

"Nice to meet you, Virgil. Bram's been singing your praises back there. Where'd you play?"

Virgil's eyes widened at hearing his name coming out of Martin's mouth, and it took a moment before he remembered that he needed to answer him.

"Centre-back, sir. Well, I've been playing right-back as well, and I can play at left … "

Martin cut him off.

"That's fine, but where do you WANT to play?"

"Centre-back," Virgil replied without hesitating.

"Then that's where we'll put you. Next Saturday we're doing trials for players. Only supposed to be a select group mind, but I think I can find a place for you. You up for it?"

Virgil nodded frantically, a wide smile breaking out across his face.

"Excellent! See you there. I must be off now."

As Bram led his guest back toward the restaurant, Martin stealthily turned and gave Virgil a smile and a quick 'thumbs up'.

Energised by what had just happened, Virgil swiped his hand across the water in the sink, splashing it over himself and the walls.

He had just been given another chance.

5
GRONINGEN

Early May 2011
Groningen training ground, Groningen

Virgil collapsed to his knees, panting desperately. He reached for his water and squirted it all over his face.

"Up you get, son. We've got another drill to do!"

Virgil staggered to his feet, turned and sprinted to join the other players preparing for their next running drill.

He'd secured a spot in Groningen's squad and,

working his way up, he'd been training with their first team for almost a year now. He was itching to make his debut, but the fitness requirements were unlike anything he'd ever experienced before.

Their next game was against ADO Den Haag and it was a crucial one. The players muttered that this must be why their manager, Pieter Huistra, was watching their drills today. Pieter didn't usually pay this much attention to routine fitness training.

When the training finally came to an end, Pieter beckoned Virgil over to him.

Virgil obediently jogged straight over with all the energy he could muster and stood breathing heavily in front of his manager.

"Everything alright?" he wheezed.

"Catch your breath, Virgil," Pieter chuckled. "You might want to brace yourself for this."

Virgil's body tensed. At seventeen he'd already experienced his fair share of rejection letters. He'd be gutted to find himself back in the position he was in before Martin had given him this chance at Groningen.

"Right, you've been with us a while and we've all been very impressed. I think the major concern with you has been your stamina, but … " he paused, looking Virgil up and down. "But, I think you're ready. I'm putting you in the squad for the Den Haag game. If it's going well, you'll get 20 minutes."

Virgil was stunned. Suddenly the emotion swept over him. He was actually going to be a professional footballer for a team in the Eredivisie!

He instantly made himself a promise. He promised that this 20 minutes against Den Haag would be the best 20 minutes of football he had in him. He would make *every second* count.

"Uh, Virgil?" His manager's voice brought him back to reality and Virgil realised he hadn't said anything for several minutes.

"Yes, yes, I'm good! Thank you! Thank you so much! I won't let you down!" he babbled.

Virgil sat on the bench, soaking up the atmosphere. It wasn't a huge stadium, but compared to where he'd been before, playing for a crowd of 15,000 people was simply incredible.

The game seemed to zip past in a flash. Goals flew in at both ends, and by the 70th minute Groningen were 4-2 up. Virgil could barely remember who had scored, and he tried to focus on getting his own legs moving as he jogged up and down the touchline, warming up.

"Virgil! Get back here! You're on!"

He immediately sprinted back to the dugout and peered across the pitch. Both the centre-backs seemed to be moving OK and both had done well all afternoon. Surely the manager wasn't taking one of them off? It just didn't add up.

Pieter slapped him on the back as Virgil wrestled his bib off.

"Right, you're going on up top. Striker, yeah? Andersson's got a knock and you're a big lad. I want you in their faces, winning headers, closing down, OK?"

Virgil nodded as he tried to process his situation. He'd played as a striker before, back in the Academy at Willem, but that was years ago.

"If you get a chance, have a shot. You've got nothing to lose, big man."

The referee blew his whistle, allowing the sub to be made. Andersson trudged over, wasting a bit of time and attracting some abuse from the home fans.

As they shook hands and crossed each other, Andersson murmured to Virgil.

"You see that number four there? Put a bit of pressure on him. He's been struggling in the air all game, and you're twice my size."

Virgil looked over to where he'd gestured and jogged over, doing a couple of jumps in the air as he covered the ground.

Minutes later, a long ball over the top was coming in his direction. Virgil went for it, shrugging off the defender and leaping into the air. He made contact and flicked the ball towards the winger on the far side.

Several more times the ball was launched towards him, and each time Virgil remembered his promise to himself. Each time he harnessed all the adrenaline rushing through his body to muscle the defender away and meet the ball with a powerful header.

The game was tight and no chances fell his way, but the feeling of being out on the pitch for the first time at that level was unlike any other.

At the final whistle, Groningen were the winners. It was a vital moment for their European push and Virgil felt immense pride, knowing that he'd played a part in it.

Pieter came striding across the pitch, beaming.

"Great display, Virgil! I know that's not your natural position, but you were a real force up there today. Now, go and clap the fans. They've come a long way for this."

Giddy with praise, Virgil bounded over to where the away fans were sitting and joined the other players in giving them a round of applause.

He could see that most of the fans didn't really recognise him, but they cheered the team all the same.

He hoped that, by the end of the season, they'd all know his name.

6
THE ATTACKING DEFENDER

Late May 2011
Groningen training ground, Groningen

After his first appearance against ADO Den Haag, sub appearances were starting to establish Virgil as an impact player off the bench for Groningen.

His naturally defensive nature combined with his dominant physical presence were causing opposition defenders all sorts of problems.

Attacking positions weren't his normal role, but

Virgil didn't mind. What mattered was being on the pitch as much as possible.

Groningen's next game was going to be a real challenge. Their last encounter with old rivals ADO Den Haag had ended up with Groningen getting hammered 5-1 in the first leg of a cup tie, and Virgil had spent the whole of that game looking on from the bench.

This was Groningen's opportunity to make amends back at their home ground, and Virgil wanted to be part of it.

Virgil met with his manager before the game.

Pieter had grown fond of Virgil ever since he'd been brought through the door by Martin Koeman. He considered him to be a good mix – someone who had a natural talent for the sport, but who was a hard worker, too.

And likewise, Virgil was fond of Pieter. Pieter had put a lot of trust in him in a way that other managers such as Edwin never had.

"Virgil, I'm going to start you tomorrow. I know most

people think it's over, but if we manage an early goal I think we can get something."

By the second half Groningen had indeed taken that early lead and were 1-0 up. Then they were awarded a free kick, and the lads stood around the ball, trying to work out who was going to take it.

"I'm having it!" Virgil roared, grabbing the ball and placing it down. The other players stepped back.

"You better not miss," one of them said as he moved away, but the warning fell on deaf ears.

Virgil was planning the perfect kick. He wanted to strike the ball hard with the inside of his right foot and whip it into the top right-hand corner.

He made his move, but he didn't catch the ball completely cleanly. He saw the goalkeeper scrambling across the goal, looking almost certain to catch it, when it slipped just under him and trickled over the line.

GOAL!

It was Virgil's first goal in professional football, and it was such a strange feeling for him. To a defender, the word 'goal!' usually means you haven't done your job properly.

He raised his arms in celebration and sprinted over to his team-mates and the fans. They still needed three more goals, so there was a lot left for them to do.

The game was quickly back underway.

Both teams scored early in the second half, and the game was end-to-end throughout, with Virgil barely able to catch his breath before he found himself flying into the next challenge.

And then, amidst the chaos, the ball fell to Virgil's feet and he found himself bearing down on goal.

The keeper rushed out, arms wide, but Virgil put his head down and smashed the ball as hard as he could with his left foot. The ball shot past the keeper into the bottom corner.

Virgil wheeled away towards the corner flag as the stadium erupted. Groningen were leading 4-1 and were now just a goal away from doing the impossible and levelling the tie.

When the ref then awarded them a penalty, the whole stadium froze.

This needed to be a goal.

Virgil was on for a hat-trick, but taking it himself

didn't even occur to him. Instead, he handed the ball to top scorer, Tim Matavž.

The experienced striker slammed it down the middle, handing Groningen a 5-1 lead.

"Let's win this now!" bellowed team-mate Dušan Tadić in Virgil's ear, as they leapt on to Matavž in front of the fans.

The goal had put the score at 6-6 on aggregate, and thirty minutes of extra time loomed. As the referee blew for full time, Virgil hobbled over to the manager, Pieter.

"Boss, I've got to come off," he huffed. "I can't do any more. Sorry."

Pieter nodded. "Don't worry about it. You've done fantastic!"

Virgil slumped onto the bench, exhausted, and watched the game go to penalties. With a heavy heart, Virgil watched his team lose out.

It had been a magnificent effort by the Groningen players and the fans showed their appreciation. Virgil limped over and joined the team.

No matter how well he played, losing never sat well

with him. But, as he looked out over the stadium, he only felt more determined not to let it happen again.

Next season would be *their* season.

7
HEROES

October 2011, Euroborg Stadium, Groningen
Groningen v Feyenoord

One-nil! Less than a minute into the game and Groningen were already in the lead.

"You owe me one, Dušan!" Virgil shouted, laughing. "I put that on a plate for you!"

Virgil had to pinch himself. He was playing against Feyenoord, a team he had admired when he was growing up. He was pretty sure his mum still had some of his knock-off Feyenoord shirts from when he was younger.

Dušan jokingly pushed him as he came over. "Leave off, Virgil! That was all me!"

Virgil knew that Pieter had actually brought him on to stop the striker Guidetti and, as the game unfolded, he did just that. Guidetti was the best striker in the league, but in this game he hadn't even had a sniff.

And even though in this game Virgil was back playing in a defensive position, with two minutes remaining he found himself with the ball at his feet, 35 yards from goal.

A calm voice in his head said, "Why not?" So he did. He hammered the ball and watched it whip off the wet turf and rocket past the helpless keeper.

GOAL!

Andersson was the first to reach him and he wrapped his arms around Virgil's neck as he leapt onto his back.

"You sure you're not a striker, mate?" he bellowed in Virgil's ear.

The atmosphere was deafening as Groningen's 6-0 victory was sealed.

As he stood taking it all in, he felt a presence behind him and he turned. The face he was looking at was one he'd seen so many times before on TV. It was Ronald Koeman, one of his childhood heroes and the current Feyenoord manager.

"So you're the player my dad is boasting about finding, huh?" Koeman said, as he looked him up and down. "I hate to say it, but you were exceptional out there. I don't know how you do it. You don't seem to be moving with any urgency, but somehow you're always in the way."

Starstruck, Virgil shrugged his shoulders.

"I learned from the best," he eventually replied. "I used to watch you at Barcelona all the time when I was a kid. It was my dream to play at the Nou Camp."

"Keep this up and you could be there sooner than you think," Koeman shouted over his shoulder, as he walked on to console his players – the players Virgil had just defeated.

8
NOT HERE

March 2012
Groningen training ground, Groningen

"One word for you: Ajax. You've caught Ajax's attention, mate!" Virgil's teammate Dušan exclaimed. The pair were warming up together as they always did, gently jogging back and forth between cones.

Virgil's career at Groningen was going from strength to strength. He no longer struggled with the fitness requirements, he was gaining invaluable experience, he had more goals under his belt and he was a favourite with the fans.

"Seriously. I heard they might be making a bid for you," Dušan continued.

Attention from big clubs like Ajax was unthinkable to Virgil, and he was busy contemplating just what it might mean when he suddenly stopped in his tracks and doubled over.

Dušan turned round to look at him.

"You alright?" he asked. The colour had drained from Virgil's face – a face that was now contorted in pain. A group of his team mates huddled round him and he heard one of them shout for the team physio.

A physio came rushing over and knelt down next to him.

"Hey, Virgil, can you tell me where the pain is?"

Virgil gestured towards his stomach and groaned, unable to utter even a single word. As he focused on his breathing, he heard a stray word in a muttered discussion between the physio and the coaching staff: "ambulance".

In no time he was being hoisted into the back of one.

The paramedic murmured some words of reassurance, but the words were wasted. By then, Virgil was barely conscious.

He couldn't bear to look at this white ceiling any more. Earlier that same day, he'd been preparing for a full season in the Dutch first division, and now here he was, stuck in a hospital with no idea what was wrong with him. He'd not felt himself for a while, but he'd assumed it was just a bug of some kind.

He heard the sound of the door being pushed open and saw his mum bundling in, followed by the doctor. After a frantic three-hour drive to get to the hospital, Hellen looked just as haggard as her son.

The doctor was the first to speak.

"Sorry for the wait, Virgil, but we've run the tests and we think we know what the problem is. You've got a case of kidney poisoning. You're lucky you are in such excellent physical condition, otherwise you might not be sitting here right now."

The doctor paused to let the words sink in.

Not here? The possibility of 'not here' was terrifying and Virgil couldn't help but feel grateful for the gruelling drills Groningen had made him do, day after day.

"Treatment is slow – your body has to fight the poison – but now that we've caught it, you'll be OK."

Virgil nodded slowly. It was a lot to take in and he didn't quite know what to say. The first thing that came to his mind was the first thing that *always* came to his mind.

"When will I be able to play football again?"

He saw his mum, standing behind the doctor, roll her eyes. She was just happy to hear her son's voice, even if he was still rambling on about football.

The doctor chuckled.

"Let's just start the first course of treatment and then we can take it step by step. First, we'll work out when you can leave the hospital. Playing football will come later."

His mum came over and gave him a hug.

"Oh Virg, don't worry about the football, you idiot! Just focus on getting better and we'll go from there."

Virgil frowned. *Of course* he wanted to get better, but

Groningen releasing him from his contract was now a real possibility.

Mistaking his frown as a response to the pain, Hellen took his hand and held it tight, just like she used to do when he was hurting from his growing pains, all those years ago.

Eventually, he managed to fall asleep.

Five days and nights passed with no word from Groningen. Did that mean bad news? Were they just waiting a while before giving him the bad news he feared?

As much as Virgil was shaken by the events of the last week, and as much as he wanted to focus on his health, he couldn't get football out of his mind. He knew that, with every day he was stuck in the hospital bed, his strength was waning. All the fitness that he'd worked on over the previous season and the summer was just falling away.

There was a knock on the door.

"Come in," Virgil said weakly. Now his voice didn't even sound like his own.

He peered over, expecting another nurse, but instead saw Pieter.

"Well, this looks pretty awful, doesn't it? How are you feeling, son?"

"It's not too bad. I'm sure I'll be back on the pitch in no time, though."

Pieter laughed and affectionately ruffled Virgil's hair.

"I'm sure you will be." Pieter paused. "But look, I've come here to tell you there's no rush. You focus on getting yourself fit and healthy, and we'll do everything we can to support you. And don't worry, Virgil. Your position at the club is safe. You mum was keen for you to know that."

It was exactly what he needed to hear.

9
RECOVERY

June 2012

Groningen training ground, Groningen

Virgil was sick of treadmills. Nevertheless, day after day, he made his way down to the gym to continue his rehab.

He took a deep gulp of air through the oxygen mask. It had been four weeks since he'd been released from hospital, and now he was desperate to get back out on the pitch.

The physio tapped a button on the treadmill and it slowed to a halt.

"Another good session," he remarked encouragingly.

"Thanks, man, but any idea when I can get back out on the pitch? These sessions are fine and all, but I need to be playing football again." Virgil steadily stepped off the machine. "I mean ... that's what I do."

"Virgil, anyone else in your position would be thankful they're alive, not trying to play football again in under a month. Recovery takes time."

Disappointment flashed across Virgil's face.

"But having said that ... I think we might be able to get you out on the training pitch. You have made exceptional progress."

It was true. When he'd left the hospital, Virgil had been barely able to walk 10 metres without struggling for breath, but now he was able to jog a fair distance quite comfortably.

It was the news he'd been waiting for and he was elated.

Within a few days the ball was back at his feet. He started with one-on-one sessions with a coach. Together they worked on passing the ball longer distances, as well as practising headers and jumping. He was regaining his strength, his agility and his feel for the ball. At last, he was back doing what he loved.

And a few weeks later, to the astonishment of everyone, he started preseason training with the first team.

He took the ball off Matavž, went on a mazy run up the field and laid the ball off to Dušan, who smacked it into the net.

"Maybe I need to spend some time in hospital, too. It's clearly worked for you!" Dušan joked, as he high-fived Virgil.

Virgil smiled at his friend and secretly agreed. If anything, he felt better than he had before. Now he was hungry – and ready to take his football to the next level.

10
OLD FRIENDS, NEW PLANS

March 2013

Euroborg Stadium, Groningen

The new season had seen a lot of changes at Groningen. Pieter had been replaced as manager by Robert Maaskant and some of Virgil's closest friends at the club had left, including Dušan. He had joined their rivals, FC Twente, who Groningen were now due to play.

This was a match that Virgil was itching to win, and not just because he'd love to beat his old friend.

Since his illness he'd really felt as if he'd come back stronger, and he'd already had a promising preseason behind him.

Now he wanted everyone to know what he was made of.

When his defensive partner and club captain Kees Kwakman pulled him aside before the game, Virgil assumed it just was to talk about tactics.

"Look, the gaffer says I'm not going to start today," Kees told him. "He asked me who I thought should be captain, and I told him I thought it should be you."

Virgil was almost speechless. It was a huge honour to lead his team out, and what made it even sweeter for him was that nobody even questioned it. He was barely 21 years old and, even though there were far more experienced players in the side, they all accepted him as captain.

Out on the pitch he saw Dušan's familiar face and went over to him.

"I hope you're going to try and stop me this time, Virgil," laughed Dušan as they embraced.

Groningen had already played Twente once this

season and it had been a heavy defeat for Groningen, with Dušan scoring twice.

"You'll see once we get out there, mate," grinned Virgil, as he turned and jogged towards his side of the pitch.

Virgil worked hard all game, but the team just couldn't pull it together and make any goals happen. Twente, however, played well.

When Dušan stepped up to take a penalty, Virgil stood behind him and tried to throw him off.

"We all know which way you're going to go," he taunted.

"Good luck with that – I'm not even sure myself which way I'm going," laughed Dušan, before smashing the ball into the back of the net.

Full time saw Groningen losing the game 3-0. It weighed heavily on Virgil as he trudged toward the touchline. Dušan jogged over to him.

"You need to get out of there, mate. You're far too good for Groningen now," Dušan panted, as he walked down the tunnel alongside Virgil.

Virgil knew that the team was struggling to make

much progress in any of their campaigns, no matter how well he played. And it was starting to feel frustrating that any success they did have always seemed to be totally dependent on his solid partnership with Kees at the back.

"I don't know. They gave me my start in football – I can't just leave."

"Listen, Virgil," Dušan replied carefully. "You're good enough to play in England or Spain, but you're not going to do that if you spend the next 10 years at Groningen!"

II
DECISIONS

May 2013

Groningen training ground, Groningen

It pained Virgil to admit it, but he knew that Dušan was right. Another stuttering end to Groningen's season meant that they only just made it to the Europa League playoffs. He'd loved his time with the club, but he wanted to go further than that.

Sitting in his manager's office, he voiced how he'd been feeling ever since the conversation with his friend.

"I obviously don't want to cause any trouble, Robert, but I do want to hand in a transfer request."

The manager paused for what seemed like an age before he replied. He spoke slowly, as if he was choosing his words extremely carefully.

"I understand, Virgil. Obviously I want you to stay, but I won't make you. We've already had some interest in you, to be totally honest. A couple of clubs have enquired – Ajax, here in Holland, and Celtic in Scotland."

Ever since he was a kid, it had been Virgil's dream to play for Ajax. Could it actually come true? And what about Celtic? Moving his footballing career to a whole other country sounded just as incredible, too.

Sensing his indecision, Maaskant spoke again.

"Look, Virgil. I'm not expecting you to say any more right now. I'll let the club know you want to leave, and we'll see if anyone makes a firm offer. Now, go and get some time off. You've earned it."

In the following days Virgil agonised over which club might be the right choice for him. He wanted to be prepared for when an offer came through, but he soon realised it was going to be a tough decision.

Everyone he asked for advice seemed to have a different opinion. His agent wanted one thing and the club wanted another.

Some of his team-mates warned him how tough it could be, moving abroad, while others said it was his chance to build his profile in a new country. Virgil knew that both of those things were probably true, but it didn't help him with the choice at hand.

He also knew that, though his mum would prefer him close to home, she just wanted whatever made him happy. He just had to work out what that was.

But the longer he thought about it, the more confused he felt – and he was no nearer to deciding what he wanted to do.

Lying in bed that night, he thought back to what he would have wanted when he was younger. He found himself thinking of the park near his childhood home, where he and his little friends used to play. He could vividly remember where they would lay their rolled-up coats to mark out goals, and he smiled at the memory.

Then, it clicked. He loved Ajax, but he'd already been playing here in Holland for a couple of years. Scotland offered a totally different game in a totally different country, and he was sure he'd come out of it a better player.

And, when it came down to it, that's actually what he'd always wanted … to be one of the greats.

When a bid finally came in from Celtic, he didn't hesitate. Ajax turned out not to be interested anyway, and, as Virgil boarded the flight to Glasgow, he looked forward to making them regret it.

12
CELTIC

July 2013
Celtic training ground, Glasgow, Scotland

As Virgil walked into the training ground's canteen, he was conscious of all the other players' eyes on him.

For these first two weeks after his arrival at Celtic, they'd all kept their distance. It seemed as if they just didn't like him at all.

Being the new guy was just one of the things Virgil was having to get used to – and fast. Another was the miserable weather. Holland had hardly been a warm country but, for Virgil, compared to Scotland it was practically tropical.

But there were positive differences, too. As some people had warned him, the style of football in Scotland was very different. In Holland it was about keeping the ball at all costs. But here they wanted to get the ball forward quickly, by any means possible, and put pressure on defenders.

This actually suited Virgil, and he was already winning headers and flying into challenges as if he'd been playing in the UK for years.

Even so, he was constantly aware that he was a long way from Breda. Luckily, there was another Dutch player at Celtic – Derk Boerrigter – and Virgil spent a lot of time with him, both on and off the training pitch. Together they messed around, played FIFA and laughed about the many times they'd struggled to understand the Scottish accent.

It was just enough to take the edge off missing home.

Virgil saw Derk sitting in the canteen and stepped over to join him. Then, as he was picking at the strange-tasting food, Virgil felt a tap on his shoulder. He turned to find himself face-to-face with a couple of the Scottish lads that had been keeping their distance.

"Virgil, is it? I hear you're supposed to be some kind of Dutch superstar. How come I never heard of ya?" one of them boomed.

Virgil blinked, unsure of how to respond, as the player stared him down.

"Nae worry! I'm just kidding, lad! You're not like most of the other Dutch players we get – they're normally tiny little fellas like Derk here!"

Then he laughed, sticking out a hand – which Virgil shook. "It's good to have you, Virgil!" he added.

Some of the other Scottish players made their way over and joined the conversation. Virgil found out a bit about them, told them a bit about himself and laughed at their banter. It meant a lot to just feel like one of the lads again.

"Van Dijk!"

The banter stopped and Virgil turned as he heard his name echo through the canteen area. It was one of the coaches, but Virgil didn't have a clue what he was saying.

"The manager wants to see you right now," Derk translated with a knowing smile.

Celtic's manager, Neil Lennon, was sitting behind his desk flicking through some papers when Virgil sat down. Unsmiling, he looked up.

"Right, Virgil. Welcome to the club – I don't think we've met properly yet, have we?"

Virgil shook his head, expecting a warm hello – that didn't come.

"I've been impressed by you in training and from what I've seen before, in Holland. I'm going to give you a few minutes against Aberdeen next week, then I'm expecting you to be my main centre-back."

Virgil nodded, now matching Neil's serious expression.

It felt as if he was about to be quizzed on the club. Luckily, he'd spent a lot of time researching Celtic and knew a fair bit about them.

"We need leaders and winners here, Virgil. I need to know now – do you have what it takes?"

"I'm here to win trophies," Virgil said calmly. It was the truth.

"Excellent. Now get back out there!"

Virgil got up to leave the brief meeting and, as he did so, Neil made one more remark.

"Oh, and Virgil, make sure you enjoy your time here in Scotland. Because if you're half as good as I think you are, you won't be here for long."

13
REALITY CHECK

December 2013, Nou Camp, Barcelona, Spain
Celtic v Barcelona

To be playing Barcelona at the Nou Camp in front of 90,000 people was incredible.

This was a pitch on which Virgil had watched countless games as a child, when Dutch superstars like Ronald Koeman and Marc Overmars were playing for Barcelona.

And now he was here, at a place he sometimes

thought he'd never get to see in real life, let alone actually play a match in.

Over the past five months, Virgil had become a vital part of Celtic's team, and he'd formed a good partnership with Efe Ambrose at the back. But now they were here, trying to hold their own against a Barcelona side who just happened to be one of the best in Europe.

The ground seemed to shake with the noise of all the Barcelona fans as Virgil followed his team out onto the pitch. He glanced around the stadium, completely in awe of the size of it.

It felt like barely minutes later that Virgil was trudging back into the dressing room at half-time. The game had been played at a ridiculously high pace and he was disappointed with his performance.

With Barcelona already leading 3-0, what had started out feeling like a dream had become a nightmare. Virgil hadn't got anywhere near Neymar or Sanchez, both of whom led the line for Barcelona.

After improving so much in recent months, it was a serious reality check for Virgil about how far he still had to go to reach the top.

"Sorry, Efe," he mumbled to his teammate. "I know I've not been good enough today."

Efe laughed. "Don't be so hard on yourself. Just be thankful we don't have to play them again for another year, at least!"

But Virgil wasn't comforted. Even though Celtic had been flying through the Scottish season and were top of the league – without losing a single game – he couldn't shake his frustration. When he played badly, he was letting down all those people who had put faith in him; people who had said he was right to leave Groningen, people who were now saying he might be too good for Celtic.

Evidently, they were wrong.

Sensing his partner's uncharacteristic dip in mood, Efe leaned in and looked at Virgil. His voice was serious.

"It's all very well being able to kick a ball, Virgil. But you'll find it's a lot more important that you know how to kick any self-doubt. You're still so young. Just watch what these players do – and take this chance to learn close-up from the very best."

In the second half, back on the pitch, Virgil watched how the likes of Neymar and Sanchez moved. He needed to learn how to stop them – not just for this match, but so that he could become a better player.

Here, they were still too quick for him and the game continued in the same way as the first half, with Barcelona running out 6-1 winners.

At full time, Virgil shook hands with the Barcelona players.

"This is the closest I've got to you all game!" he joked to Neymar, who had scored a hat-trick in the match.

Neymar laughed and wished him luck, before moving on. Virgil watched him go and, with Efe's words in his head, decided that the next time he faced him, he'd be the one with a smile on his face.

14
THE BOOKING

February 2014, Pittodrie Stadium, Aberdeen, Scotland
Celtic v Aberdeen

The word 'unbeaten' was something Virgil took immense pride in saying. And although Celtic had been thumped by Barcelona in the Champions League, they were yet to taste defeat in the Scottish League.

The atmosphere within the stadium rivalled that of the Nou Camp, despite it being less than half the size, and Virgil knew that tonight they were going to be in for a difficult evening. Aberdeen were the only side with the potential to catch them.

Just 15 minutes in and a poor pass from left-back Charlie Mulgrew allowed an Aberdeen striker to get away one-on-one. Virgil sprinted after him and quickly managed to get level.

Seeing a flash of the yellow ball between the Aberdeen player's legs, he made a decision and dived in. The Aberdeen player had anticipated this and was ahead of Virgil, poking the ball away with his right foot. Virgil collided with the player's leg, leaving the player crumpled on the floor.

In what seemed like slow motion, the ref jogged over and reached into his pocket, producing a red card.

Virgil had no complaints about the decision and quickly returned to the dressing room alone.

When the players piled back in at half-time, they confirmed what he had suspected from the roars of the crowd and the rumbling he could feel through the floor: Aberdeen were 2-0 up.

He sat quietly while the manager gave a quick team talk, before sending them back on their way.

Neil paused, remaining behind as the team went out. He turned to where Virgil was sitting, his head hanging in shame.

"Don't be too hard on yourself, lad. You were put in a difficult position. Maybe next time don't dive in unless you're 100% sure you can get the ball. You've got the pace – you could have got back onside and blocked the shot instead. Making the right decisions only comes with a lot of experience."

Virgil gave his boss a small smile.

"Seriously. Don't worry about the red card, Virgil. We're going to win the league and that's all that people will remember. Not whether we went the season unbeaten."

He marched back out to the touchline and left Virgil with his thoughts.

Neil was right. Barely two months later, Virgil was climbing on to a bus ready for the trophy parade through the centre of Glasgow. The streets were lined with thousands of fans and all Virgil could see was a sea of green and white.

He felt a slap on his shoulder and turned to find Scott Brown handing him the trophy. It was the first of his professional career.

"Go on, Virgil, give it a lift! You've earned it!"

Virgil took the trophy and raised it high above his head. The crowd erupted.

As well as being named Celtic's Player of the Season, beating Kris Commons and Scott Brown, he had also been nominated for Player of the Season in Scotland.

"VIRGIL! VIRGIL!"

He tried to capture this moment, to file it all away in his memory, so he could come back to it and enjoy it again and again.

Passing the trophy on to the next player, he beamed and applauded the city he had come to think of as a home.

But despite how comfortable he was in Scotland, Virgil's thoughts inevitably turned to the Netherlands, as a month later the 2014 World Cup got underway in Brazil.

Holland were involved in a tough opening game against Spain, and Virgil and a few of the Celtic players met up to watch the match on TV.

Virgil looked at the familiar names of Robin van Persie and Arjen Robben lining up for the national side.

A small part of him had hoped that after this season with Celtic he might have got a call-up, but he'd had no contact from Dutch team manager Louis van Gaal.

As the players came out, he saw that Stefan de Vrij and Bruno Martins-Indi were both part of the Dutch defence. He'd played against them barely a year earlier, when they had been at Feyenoord. It felt tough to accept that they'd been picked over him.

But as the match got underway, his mood quickly changed. Holland ran out 5-1 winners, completely stunning the Spanish team – and most of the world.

"I don't think we're ever going to get in the team now," joked Derk, as they watched the players celebrating.

"Ah, speak for yourself," Virgil jested with a wink.

15
A GREAT RESULT

February 2015, Celtic Park Stadium, Glasgow
Celtic v Inter Milan

Iceland, Poland and Slovenia. Virgil had barely travelled out of Holland before joining Celtic, but now he was travelling to many different and distant places.

But now their opponents, Inter Milan, were flying to Scotland for an away game, and Virgil was ready for them. He'd been working as hard as ever in training, with Celtic's new manager Ronny Delia encouraging him to take more risks. Virgil found himself dribbling more, passing more and becoming very influential when Celtic were on the attack.

"It's like Messi and John Terry had a baby! Is there anything you can't do?" Teemu Pukki had exclaimed in training, after Virgil had won the ball with a firm challenge and then dribbled past three players.

The atmosphere was electric as the players lined up in the tunnel. There was no Champions League anthem, but the Celtic fans made up for that with their own songs and chants. Amongst the Celtic fans, the feeling that their team could win this game was tangible.

But after 25 minutes, quick goals from Xherdan Shaqiri and Rodrigo Palacio had put Inter 2-0 up.

"Come on!" bellowed Virgil "We can sort this out. Just start playing properly!"

Virgil had a natural sense of what his team-mates needed to hear and, as usual, his words hit home. Celtic began to improve. Stuart Armstrong pulled a goal back, before forcing an Inter defender into conceding an own goal. It was now 2-2!

"That one was for you, man!" Stuart shouted.

"What do you mean?" Virgil replied.

"I was so scared you were going to yell at me again. I've never seen you that angry!"

The pair grinned at each other and Virgil fiercely led the team up to the final whistle. It was 3-3 and everyone on the team erupted in celebration – except Virgil, who held back. A 3-3 draw at home wouldn't be enough to send them through.

Stuart came over to celebrate with him at full time.

"What a result, huh, Virgil?" he grinned.

"But we drew at home. And we conceded three. They're probably going to beat us in the second leg. We won't go through."

"And? They're a better team! This is a great result for us!" he shouted, sprinting off to join in the celebrations with some of the other players.

It wasn't the first time Virgil had felt that there was a difference in what 'a great result' meant for Celtic and what it meant for himself.

16
WORD FROM SOUTHAMPTON

August 2015
Virgil's home, Glasgow

The sound of Virgil's TV almost drowned out the buzzing of his phone next to him. Luckily, he saw the screen light up in the corner of his eye. It read *Unknown number*, which sparked his interest. Virgil was very careful about who got to know his phone number.

He flicked off the TV and accepted the call.

"Hello?"

"Yo, Virgil, it's Dušan – Dušan Tadić. We played together at Groningen."

Virgil's face cracked into a wide smile at Dušan's familiar voice. He sounded just as he had done when they were younger.

"Of course! What's up, mate?"

They had lost touch with each other, but Virgil knew that Dušan was now playing in England with Southampton.

"I've just been hearing your name a lot round here, and thought we should catch up."

"My name? At Southampton?"

"You bet. Koeman is in charge here now – and he remembers you from Holland."

The conversation quickly turned to memories of their time in Holland, and the two reminisced about their old lives and how things had changed.

But all the while Virgil's mind was racing. Ronald Koeman, his hero, remembered him … He thought back to their first encounter in Holland and how dumb he must have looked, all wide-eyed and startled to see this man in person.

Even in bed, long after his conversation with Dušan, Virgil lay awake thinking about what he'd said. Virgil now had a second trophy with Celtic under his belt, and he had loved playing for the club.

But, if he was honest with himself, he just didn't feel settled there. He knew he could take his football further.

The next day, Virgil went in to his manager's office to speak to Ronny Deila. Before he even got a word out, the manager interrupted him.

"Let me guess. This is about Southampton."

Virgil nodded, waiting with bated breath to hear what the manager had to say next.

"They've made an offer for you … "

17
THE CALL-UP

October 2015

Southampton training ground, Southampton, England

"Does the name Danny Blind ring any bells?" Southampton manager Ronald Koeman teased Virgil as he was jogging in from another hard training session with the Saints.

He'd only been with them a couple of weeks, but he was elated to see how much his football had improved in that time.

Virgil stopped in his tracks and his mouth dropped open.

"Wait. Are you saying what I think you're saying?"

Koeman nodded and Virgil punched the air, at the same time giving out a "Whoop!" of excitement.

Danny Blind, the manager of the Netherlands team, had been on the phone. That could only mean one thing: Virgil was being called up to play for his national team.

This was what he had heard so many players call the pinnacle of their career, the ultimate achievement: playing for your country at the highest level.

Yet Virgil just couldn't process the fact it was happening to him! He'd thought about playing for his country before, of course, but this news seemed to come out of nowhere.

He'd known that Holland were looking for players to help them move forward after some dreadful results, but he hadn't known that he was top of their list, after his impressive first few games at Southampton.

Some of his new team-mates and other members of staff came over to congratulate him. He giddily thanked them and started making a mental list of who he wanted to call and share the news with.

A few days later, he was standing in Kazakhstan, making his debut for a Dutch national team that was vastly underperforming.

Virgil felt instantly at home within their ranks, despite playing alongside players who had much more experience than him.

Early in the game, he quickly fell into a leadership role he felt very comfortable in, marshalling the defence against a tough Kazakhstani attack in front of a vocal home crowd.

"Concentrate!"

He was yelling at players who'd been in the national side for much longer than him.

"Robin! Watch your man!" he cautioned van Persie, as the Dutch held on for a 2-1 win.

"Wow, it feels as if you've been in our defence for years!" shouted Wesley Sneijder, as they stood on the pitch and celebrated the win.

"Boss you cannot *ever* drop this man," midfielder Gini Wijnaldum muttered to Danny Blind afterwards.

18
SAINT VIRGIL

October 2015, Anfield Stadium, Liverpool
Liverpool v Southampton

Yet again, Virgil was part of a team that was on an unbeaten run.

It had been a good feeling at Celtic, but here at Southampton, in the Premier League, it was a phenomenal feeling. The Saints had won their last six games, and Virgil had scored twice.

Now the team were preparing to take on Liverpool,

one of the biggest teams in the League, with some of the biggest names in world football at their disposal.

Nevertheless, with his impressive national debut under his belt, Virgil was confident. He knew how far he had come and he was comfortable in the belief that he could hold his own at this level.

Playing at Southampton was continuing to do wonders for his ability. He had known that the club were doing well in the league, but he hadn't quite anticipated the level of intensity at which Premier League games were played.

The pace was much higher than he'd been used to when he'd been playing in either Holland or Scotland, but he was loving being amongst this group of players who all had the same mentality as him. They used quick passes, put a lot of pressure on opposition defenders and wanted to see results.

He was also learning a lot from the players around him – knowledge that he quickly realised was giving him a better understanding of the game.

He thought back to Southampton's last away game at West Brom. It had been his first taste of Premier

League football and, for the first time in his career, Virgil had found himself struggling to beat players in the air.

He remembered hearing his centre-back partner, José Fonte, shout his name.

"Virgil! If you're not going to win the header, then you're better stepping back from them and winning the ball when it's on the floor!"

Virgil had taken José's advice. The next time the ball came over, he'd allowed Rickie Lambert to bring it down. Then, as the ball was on the floor, he'd stepped in and taken it off Rickie's toes.

At the end of that game, his first for Southampton, Virgil had felt as if he'd already learned more in 90 minutes of Premier League football than in 90 games of Scottish and Dutch football combined.

Tips like that – and so many more – were tucked away in Virgil's head as he took on Liverpool. And, to everyone's amazement, he kept Liverpool's superstar forwards – Coutinho, Firmino and Lallana – quiet.

Keeping a cool head, Virgil's passes were tight – and he even came close to scoring a goal with one of his now notorious headers.

But as the match drew to a close, it marked the end of Southampton's winning streak. They drew with Liverpool 1-1.

As ever, a draw was never a score that sat well with Virgil, no matter who the opponent was, and he was disappointed – along with the rest of his team. But there was some consolation when he was awarded Man of the Match.

As Virgil was leaving the pitch, Liverpool manager Jürgen Klopp approached him with some words of praise for his performance.

"If you hadn't have just signed for Southampton, I'd have you on my team!" he chuckled.

Virgil thanked him for the kind words, turned, and walked off the Anfield pitch with his head held high.

19
VIRGIL'S REVENGE

October 2016

Southampton training ground, Southampton

Virgil had enjoyed a full summer away from football for the first time ever, and it had cleared his mind and renewed his hunger for the game.

The European Championships had been on the TV but, with Holland missing out, they'd held no interest for him. He'd only tuned in to the final to watch his friend José help Portugal to the trophy.

At full time he'd texted José to congratulate him:

> Congrats!! You better watch out in 4 years though – the Dutch are coming back strong.

> Haha. I'll be long retired in 4 years, Virgil!

Now back on the pitch with José and thoroughly rested, Virgil wanted to be playing exciting football, so they could get back to defeating the likes of Arsenal, Manchester City and Tottenham.

But with Mauricio Pellegrino installed as the new manager at Southampton, there had been a change of tactics at the club, with a stronger focus on defence.

"Can't we just try and put a bit more into attack?" Virgil moaned to team-mate James Ward-Prowse in training. James looked at Virgil and shrugged.

Their defensive style was securing them good draws with some of the bigger teams, but they were struggling to beat the smaller ones.

As Virgil knew, getting just a point against the top teams might be OK, but only if you were collecting three points against the rest of the teams in the league.

This new defensive approach had been adopted in the Europa League as well, and Southampton were now facing elimination, with a huge game against Inter Milan looming.

Virgil remembered Inter from his time with Celtic and he was determined to get revenge, adamant that in that game Mauro Icardi had got him wrongly sent off.

He got stuck into the training sessions and worked tirelessly during every drill. He wanted to be as prepared as possible for this match.

The game started poorly, with Icardi firing Inter into an early lead and Dušan Tadić missing a penalty.

But in the second half Virgil took control of the game for his side.

"Come on lads, let's put on a performance! For the fans!"

And in a moment's reflection, he gave himself a stern talking to: *The Celtic game was then, and this is now ... I'm NOT losing to this lot again!*

As if his words were working magic, Southampton won a flurry of corners. A good save from the keeper blocked one of Virgil's efforts, but he refused to lift the pressure.

The next corner found its way to him after rebounding off the crossbar. The ball fell to his feet and he poked it straight past the keeper.

GOAL!

"Stick me on penalties as well next time, mate!" he shouted at Dušan, as they bundled into the corner flag. Dušan grinned at his long-time friend.

Southampton eventually ran out 2-1 winners on a famous night for the club, with Virgil at the centre of it.

"What a result!" shouted James Ward-Prowse. "You were immense, Virgil!"

"Now let's start doing that in the league as well!" Virgil fired back with a big grin.

20
THE RECORD-BREAKING REDS

December 2017

Southampton training ground, Southampton

"Seventy-five million?" he said in disbelief. "Seventy-five million!" he repeated. Virgil's brain just couldn't comprehend that kind of number.

"Wow!" was all he said next. The word came out sounding so quiet, so anti-climactic, that the Southampton staff sitting around the meeting table with him couldn't help but smile.

Liverpool had offered 75 million to buy him. Virgil had to keep repeating it to make it sink in.

He was overwhelmed that Liverpool would pay this kind of fee for him. He'd even picked up an injury last season and had missed a lot of games.

He asked himself, not for the first time, if they'd got this right. Perhaps there had been a mistake. Or they were playing a cruel joke on him.

Tensions were still running a little high between the three parties involved: the two clubs and himself. His thoughts went back to the phone call from Liverpool's manager, Jürgen Klopp, that had started all the drama.

"I just want to talk to you about Liverpool, and what you would think about coming to play for us," Jürgen had said to him.

It was an opportunity Virgil would have killed for, but there were also alarm bells ringing in his head. This wasn't the official way to go about approaching a player about a possible transfer from one club to another … He felt sure there were rules against it.

So he'd replied to Klopp on the phone with a vague

answer, not wanting to sound either too keen or too disinterested.

But news of his conversation with Klopp got back to Southampton and, as Virgil suspected, the phone call was considered an illegal approach. That was a serious matter.

Southampton made a complaint to the Premier League and Liverpool were forced to make a formal apology.

After all that had happened, Virgil had half-expected that Liverpool would just forget it and shelve him forever. He would have understood.

So all that made this offer from Liverpool all the more unbelievable.

Virgil turned to look at Pellegrino, who had kept a straight face throughout the meeting.

"The board have discussed it and we're happy to accept the offer. We know it's what you want, Virgil."

Virgil pressed his hands to his face.

"It's a world-record transfer fee for a defender, you know," one of the coaches chimed in.

Virgil was speechless as he accepted everyone's congratulations and praise.

In his mind's eye he could already see himself on Liverpool's training ground. He would be reunited with Sadio Mané, and would meet a host of other players who would leave him totally starstruck.

Except that now, there was an important difference. Now, Virgil could imagine some of the players looking at *him* in the same way. He was the most expensive defender in the world, and he was going to prove to the world that he was worth every penny.

21
A DREAM DEBUT

January 2018, Anfield Stadium, Liverpool
Liverpool v Everton

Virgil's name had been plastered across newspapers around the world, with many so-called 'experts' slating the price tag that had come with his move to Liverpool.

Inevitably, all eyes were going to be on him when he made his debut for his new club. What made it even more special was the fact that it was a local derby against Everton.

As the Liverpool team ran out on to the pitch, Anfield was practically rocking with excitement.

"This is nuts!" Virgil shouted over the noise to the captain, James Milner. Milner turned and gave him a big 'Welcome to Anfield' grin.

Virgil glanced over at the Everton team and realised that he recognised all of the players. This was a perk that he'd never been able to enjoy before, as in the past moving clubs had always meant moving countries – which in turn meant moving into a different league with different players.

It felt as if the Premier League had become his home.

Suddenly, Jürgen came into view and reassuringly put his hands on Virgil's shoulders.

"Maybe I'm not worth all that money," Virgil confessed, looking straight at his manager. Though his face looked composed and it was said in a joking way, Virgil's eyes betrayed a small amount of panic that Jürgen registered.

Jürgen chuckled gently and calmly replied, "I just happen to think that you are."

The game started at a breathtaking pace, with players from both sides flinging themselves into challenges. Virgil was a calming influence at the centre of this storm, helping to relax the two defenders Joe Gomez and Andrew Robertson alongside him.

As the game neared a close, it looked as if Everton were going to hold their local rivals to a draw.

A corner from Alex Oxlade-Chamberlain was one last throw of the dice from Liverpool. As the ball drifted in, Virgil hurled himself towards the ball, arriving at it seconds before Pickford. The ball cannoned off his head into the back of the net.

GOAL!

Virgil sprinted towards the corner flag, diving onto his knees and sliding across the Anfield turf. He couldn't have wished for a better start to his Liverpool career! A goal in the last minutes of the game, in his first appearance for his new club – and in a derby!

"You'll be a Liverpool legend already, mate!" Oxlade-Chamberlain bellowed to Virgil, as he punched the air in front of the Liverpool fans, who were on their feet going wild.

Barely a game in and already he felt completely at home with this club.

After bounding around the pitch in celebration, Virgil caught up with his manager. Jürgen held his hand over his mouth to obscure it from the cameras as he whispered into Virgil's ear.

"Seventy-five million seems a bargain now, doesn't it?"

He patted Virgil's back and pushed him back toward the celebrations, feeling incredibly smug as the press swarmed on to the pitch.

22
CHAMPIONSHIP CHANCES

May 2018, Kiev, Ukraine
Champions League Final, Liverpool v Real Madrid

Liverpool's focus had always been on Europe, and now they were here.

A semi-final victory over Roma had catapulted them into a final against Real Madrid, the Champions League winners for the last two years running. Superstars littered their line-up with names like Gareth Bale, Luka Modrić and Cristiano Ronaldo.

"Don't let the occasion get to you!" Jürgen said as he rallied his team in the changing rooms. "It's a game of football – and you know you can beat them."

The mood before the match was tense. Real Madrid had been here before, but Liverpool hadn't. Previous Liverpool teams had won the Champions League, but none of the current players had been a part of that.

"Just give it your best shot. Have a good time and play good football!" Klopp went on.

Virgil knew they had it in them. Their recent crushing wins over Porto and Man City had proved that their high-tempo style of football was a force to be reckoned with.

"Yeah, let's get stuck in straight away, boys," captain Jordan Henderson said, clearly stirred by his manager. "Let's keep the pressure on them."

Virgil looked around at his team-mates. He could sense that not everyone's nerves had been settled so easily. So he did what he always did, putting his friends at ease and offering up little tips they could focus on, so they didn't get caught up thinking about the bigger picture.

"Don't give them any space, alright?" he said to Dejan Lovren, his centre-back partner. "Don't show them too much respect. If they sense any weakness, they'll tear us apart."

The game started quietly, with both sides clearly in awe of the occasion. No one wanted to make the first mistake.

The first half remained uneventful, except for when Liverpool's leading scorer, Mohamed Salah, was met with a clumsy challenge. It was a nasty knock for Salah and he was taken off on a stretcher.

"There's no way we can do this without him," Lovren murmured to Virgil.

"Don't worry. Sadio is still there," Virgil said reassuringly. He knew he had to keep his team-mates calm and focused if they were going to stand any chance of winning this game.

The second half began with an error from keeper Loris Karius, and Real Madrid took a one-goal lead.

"I'm so sorry guys, I don't know what happened," he said, completely devastated.

"Loris, don't worry about it. That could have been

any one of us," Virgil replied, hoping to help his keeper stay calm and focused.

And then, out of nowhere, Sadio Mané was able to stab the ball home from a corner.

"I told you, Dejan!" Virgil bellowed over the roar of the crowd. "Always trust in Sadio!"

His joy was short-lived, however, as Gareth Bale single-handedly took the title for Real Madrid, scoring two consecutive goals that meant that they ran out 3-1 winners and took home their third consecutive Champions League title.

Collecting his runners-up medal felt like a punishment to Virgil. He wasn't used to losing with Liverpool, and he'd been so sure that this was going to be their moment.

The disappointment hung heavy over the rest of the team as well, but Jürgen was the exception. Before the players could depart the pitch, he called them all together.

"Lads, we've done so well to get this far. But, remember this feeling. Remember the feeling of getting so close, only to lose at the last moment. Because then you'll do everything in your power *never* to let it happen again."

He spoke calmly, but his voice was strong and clear. "Remember what it feels like to lose, boys. Because next year, we're coming back here and we're going to win the Champions League."

23
RIGHT BEHIND YOU

January 2019, Etihad Stadium, Manchester, England
Manchester City v Liverpool

The way Liverpool had begun the Premier League this season was being called sensational.

At the start they had gone 20 games without defeat, and by Christmas they were several points clear at the top of the league.

It was just the boost to the team's confidence that they needed, following their narrow miss in Kiev, and many said that the atmosphere in the squad had never been better.

New signings Alisson, Fabinho and Keïta were each making a substantial impact, but no one was making as big a mark as Virgil. Awarded Player of the Month multiple times, he was constantly reminding those in the world of football that, yes, he *was* worth that infamous transfer fee.

But behind all this positive news there was just one dark shadow. It was Man City. And they were hot on Liverpool's heels.

"Any other year and we'd be, like, 15 points clear at this point in the season," moaned Jordan Henderson, as the team prepared for their match against City at the Etihad.

Virgil knew that Jordan wasn't wrong, but it didn't change the facts. What mattered was *this* season, not any other season, and Liverpool now had 90 minutes to pull something out the bag against their incredibly strong opponents.

"I'd tell you to watch out for their danger man, Virgil, but that's basically their whole team!" James Milner had once joked with him in training. Lined up in the tunnel waiting to go on, the thought wasn't so funny now.

Even the atmosphere in the ground seemed different. There was a nervous tension in the air. The City fans knew that defeat for their team here could seal the title for Liverpool. But equally, all the fans in the stadium knew that a defeat for Liverpool would bring City just that bit closer.

In case anybody wasn't paying attention, Jordan Henderson made sure that they all knew what was at stake.

"Come on, boys. We can win the title tonight!"

Minutes in, and Liverpool almost took the lead, with John Stones somehow sweeping the ball off the line. Virgil couldn't believe it.

"How did that not go in?" he bellowed at Jordan Henderson, as City somehow bundled the ball clear.

"Ref said it was out by millimetres," Henderson shouted back over the roar of the crowd.

When Leroy Sané fired Man City 2-1 up in the final 20 minutes of the game, Liverpool responded by throwing everything they had at the City defence, but

Vincent Kompany's team stood firm – and at the whistle they got the result they wanted.

At the end of the game, it was Kompany who came over to Virgil, a smile on his face.

"You guys were unlucky today," he said, shaking Virgil's hand with a laugh. "I don't know *how* that one wasn't over the line!"

Virgil didn't join in the laughter. He couldn't even manage a polite smile, despite being aware that the TV cameras were on him. He was so frustrated by the game.

"You better watch your backs, though," Kompany continued. "We're right behind you now!"

24
THE IMPOSSIBLE

May 2019, Nou Camp, Barcelona, Spain
Barcelona v Liverpool

Kompany's words proved to be prophetic, although City didn't stay behind Liverpool for long.

By May, Manchester City had overtaken Liverpool and were firmly lodged at the top of the Premier League. From now until the end of the season, City were in the driving seat, and it was Liverpool who were playing catch-up.

The Champions League was a welcome distraction from the stress of the league, and it was in Europe where Liverpool were playing some of their best football.

Virgil had got his first Champions League goal for Liverpool, as well as an assist that people were calling the best pass of his career.

But now, the semi-final draw had set them up with an away game against Barcelona in the first leg.

The last time Virgil had played at the Nou Camp had been with Celtic, in one of the worst nights of his career. Unsurprisingly, he felt a few nerves about being back playing there again. This time, they were up against Lionel Messi as well.

"Any tips for facing Messi?" Virgil asked Dejan Lovren, who'd faced him at the World Cup in the previous summer.

"Just hope he has a bad day," Dejan replied with a snort.

Liverpool started poorly and their former striker, Luis Suárez, fired Barcelona into an early lead. Liverpool were definitely creating chances, but their normally clinical strikers were wasting them.

"What is going on today?" Virgil moaned to Joe Gomez, as yet another chance went wide.

Gomez looked straight at Virgil. "If we don't score, we're going out," he replied bluntly.

With 20 minutes left it looked as if Liverpool might hold on for just a 1-0 defeat.

But then Lionel Messi took control and everything changed. A rebound effort and a magnificent free kick put two more in the net and guided Barcelona to a 3-0 victory.

At the whistle the Liverpool players looked completely gutted, heads down with exhaustion and disappointment. It was Virgil who went up to all the players, reminding them that the second leg was still to come.

It wasn't over until it was over. They still had a chance, however slim.

Come match night, Anfield was deafening. Of all the huge games Virgil had been involved in, this was the loudest crowd he had ever heard. It felt as if the whole of the city of Liverpool had come out to support them in this second leg. Without a doubt it was the most inspiring noise he'd ever heard.

Even before the game had started, Liverpool had been hit by two severe blows: star attackers Firmino and Salah had both been ruled out of the game.

In their places, Divock Origi and Xherdan Shaqiri were brought into the team. Virgil sympathised with them – he knew how much pressure they must be feeling. He too felt the same pressure. The shadow of Man City pulling away from them in the Premier League was hanging over the whole team.

Virgil knew that this game, the second leg, gave him the best chance in his career so far of getting his hands on one of the major trophies he'd been dreaming about all his life. But this was a game where they were starting 3-0 down. And against Barcelona, of all teams!

Ten minutes into the game and it was Divock Origi who put Liverpool ahead. That was one goal back.

"Three more to go and we're through!" shouted Jordan Henderson. *It's not impossible*, Virgil kept telling himself, but there wasn't much evidence of that in the rest of the first half.

The second half began in a whirlwind. Gini Wijnaldum struck in the 54th minute, pulling another one back for Liverpool.

It was 2-0, 3-2 on aggregate.

Then just two minutes later, Gini struck again. Extraordinary! That was three back! Liverpool were level on aggregate and Barcelona were rattled.

"This is it, lads!" Virgil roared, driving the team on as he won the ball off Luis Suárez yet again.

The clock ticked on and the fans could barely watch when, with 10 minutes left, a clever corner from Trent Alexander-Arnold caught Barcelona napping and Divock Origi was on hand to poke the ball home.

That was four. Liverpool had taken the lead!

"Where have you been all season?" screamed Virgil, as he leapt onto Divock, dragging him to the ground.

The rest of the game was a blur. Barcelona looked completely shocked and had no answers to Liverpool's second-half onslaught.

At the whistle, the noise of the crowd inside the stadium was deafening. The Liverpool fans were celebrating a team that had done what had seemed impossible: beating Barcelona to secure a second consecutive Champions League final.

Virgil knew that moments like this were rare, and he was experienced enough now to know how to savour them.

Everything he had been dreaming of was now back within reach and, as Jürgen had said so simply last year, they were now going to go back there and win it.

They were going to go back and become kings of Europe.

25
THE BEST PLAYER IN EUROPE

December 2019, Khalifa International Stadium, Doha
Liverpool v Flamengo

One hundred and nineteen minutes into the game. Twenty-two exhausted players and Liverpool with a one-goal lead.

As one of Flamengo's attackers attempted to score an equalizer in the very last minute, Virgil made sure he was in the way to block the shot and keep the score at 1-0.

Luckily, when it came to football, Virgil's instincts were never dulled by tiredness.

Firmino had been the man to give Liverpool the lead in this hard-fought FIFA Club World Cup final, and now they just needed to keep that lead to the final whistle.

This was a title that Liverpool had never won, but their victory against Tottenham in the Champions League final had given them their chance. Virgil was not going to waste that kind of opportunity.

When the final whistle went at long last, Virgil threw his head back in relief and in celebration. For the first time in the history of the club, Liverpool had won the FIFA Club World Cup. This team had made club history!

He was soon embracing his team-mates on the pitch. They should have all been dead on their feet after such a long game, but the adrenaline of winning had kicked in and suddenly given them a new energy.

As the Liverpool fans in the stands held their scarves

in the air, Virgil stood and watched as a FIFA official approached with the trophy and officially presented it to captain Jordan Henderson.

Jordan lifted the cup high and the team, now crowded around him, cheered and waved to the fans as confetti was fired into the air behind them.

Virgil couldn't help but think about how quickly things had changed. It only felt like yesterday that he'd watched Jordan lifting the Champions League trophy. He used to spend so much time in front of that sink full of dishes in Breda, dreaming about moments like these, and now they were really happening. And, it seemed, they just kept on coming.

Because this might not be Liverpool's only trophy this season. The club had not won the Premier League for 30 years, but this year, even so early in the season, it was really beginning to look as if Liverpool could clinch it.

Liverpool had started strongly in the Premier League, just like last season. But this year they hadn't let any other teams get near them in the league, and as more games were played Liverpool just pulled further and further ahead.

Would they really be able to add the Premier League title to their season's successes, after a 30-year wait?

Virgil was suddenly struck by all he had achieved.

He'd fought for his career from the start and had refused to let anything stop him. Now here he was: the winner of multiple trophies, captain of the Dutch National team ... and officially the best player in Europe.

His mind went back to that incredible moment, last summer in Monaco, when he'd been given that title. How he'd sat with football's elite, waiting in silence as the President of UEFA had pulled open the envelope on stage and announced, "The UEFA Men's Player of the year is ... Virgil van Dijk."

Virgil had known in advance that he had won the award, but nevertheless his heart had still skipped a beat at hearing his name spoken.

As honours went, this was right up there. Cups and leagues were won by *teams*, but this award was for *him*. It was recognition of *his* personal contribution to the game.

The room had broken into polite applause as he'd pulled himself out of his seat to walk up and collect the award. This was all a far cry from the rowdy cheers of the pitch-side fans he'd come to love, but it had meant just as much.

As he'd made his way to the stage, feeling so out of place in his suit, he'd glanced sideways at the other players who had also been up for the award. Lionel Messi and Cristiano Ronaldo. Both of them had been clapping him admiringly.

Standing now in this stadium in Doha, alongside his teammates, all drenched in sweat and celebrating this great victory, Virgil smiled at the memory.

He knew these moments would stay with him forever, along with everything he had achieved on pitches all around the world.

If only that boy in Breda, anxious even about getting a professional football contract, had known that he was going to be one of the greats.

And yet he was only getting started.

HOW WELL DO YOU KNOW VIRGIL VAN DIJK?

1. What was Virgil's part-time job while he played at Willem II?
2. What position did Virgil play in his debut for Groningen?
3. What serious illness took Virgil out of action for Groningen for a couple of months?
4. Virgil led the Netherlands' team in the 2014 World Cup – true or false?
5. Who did Virgil play alongside at Groningen and Southampton?
6. Which of Virgil's childhood heroes went on to become his manager at Southampton?
7. How much did Liverpool offer for Virgil?
8. What cup did Virgil win with Liverpool in 2019, for the first time in the history of the club?

VIRGIL VAN DIJK CLUB TIMELINE

2001 – 2010   Willem II Tilburg, the Netherlands

2010 – 2013   FC Groningen, the Netherlands

2013 – 2015   Celtic F.C., Scotland

2015 – 2018   Southampton F.C., England

2018 – Present   Liverpool F.C., England

ANSWERS TO THE QUIZ OPPOSITE

1. *Dishwasher*
2. *Striker*
3. *Kidney poisoning*
4. *False – he had not yet been called up to his national team*
5. *Dušan Tadić*
6. *Ronald Koeman*
7. *75 million*
8. *FIFA Club World Cup*

HOW MANY HAVE YOU READ?

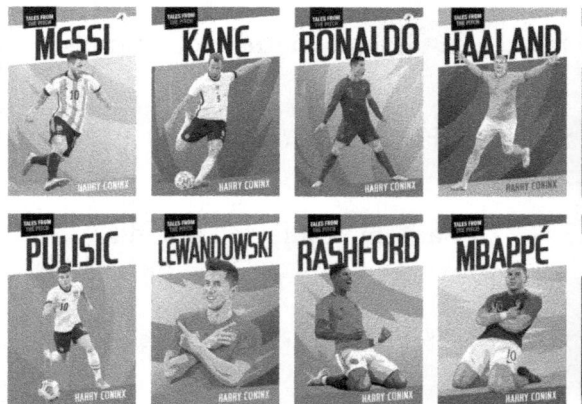

www.ingramcontent.com/pod-product-compliance
Lightning Source LLC
Chambersburg PA
CBHW022120040426
42450CB00006B/775